Chinese New Year

LEVEL O

DEC🐸DABLES BY ju🐸mp!

Teaching Tips

Lilac Level 0

This book focuses on teaching the earliest readers how to read a book by following images and text from left to right.

Before Reading

- Discuss the title. Ask readers what they think the book will be about.

Read the Book

- Encourage readers to describe what they see on each page.
- Ask questions to help readers understand the story and its progression.
  - What happens at the beginning of the book?
  - What happens at the end of the book?
  - How do we know?

After Reading

- Ask readers what part of the book they liked best. Have them find the page or pages that showed this.
- Have readers imagine a different ending for the book. What else could have happened?

North American adaptations © 2024 Jump!
5357 Penn Avenue South
Minneapolis, MN 55419
www.jumplibrary.com

Decodables by Jump! are published by Jump! Library.

Library of Congress Cataloging-in-Publication Data is available at www.loc.gov or upon request from the publisher.

ISBN: 979-8-88524-655-2 (hardcover)
ISBN: 979-8-88524-656-9 (paperback)
ISBN: 979-8-88524-657-6 (ebook)

Photo Credits

Images are courtesy of Shutterstock.com. With thanks to Getty Images, Thinkstock Photo and iStockphoto. Cover – KK Tan, JIANG HONGYAN, hareluya, Anirut Krisanakul, Tanachot Srijam, p4–5 – aslysun, elwynn, p6–7 – Toa55, windmoon, p8–9 – Tanachot Srijam, SKY2015, p10–11 – Anirut Krisanakul.

About Reading

When we read a book, we go from left to right, like this:

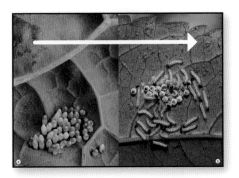

Some books just have pictures, like this:

Some books have words and pictures, like this:

Which photo shows somebody
holding something?

Making a Pizza

LEVEL 0

DEC●DABLES BY jump!

Teaching Tips

Lilac Level 0

This book focuses on teaching the earliest readers how to read a book by following images and text from left to right.

Before Reading

- Discuss the title. Ask readers what they think the book will be about.

Read the Book

- Encourage readers to describe what they see on each page.
- Ask questions to help readers understand the story and its progression.
    - What happens at the beginning of the book?
    - What happens at the end of the book?
    - How do we know?

After Reading

- Ask readers what part of the book they liked best. Have them find the page or pages that showed this.
- Have readers imagine a different ending for the book. What else could have happened?

This edition is published by arrangement with Booklife Publishing.

North American adaptations © 2024 Jump!
5357 Penn Avenue South
Minneapolis, MN 55419
www.jumplibrary.com

Decodables by Jump! are published by Jump! Library.

Library of Congress Cataloging-in-Publication Data is available at www.loc.gov or upon request from the publisher.

ISBN: 979-8-88524-655-2 (hardcover)
ISBN: 979-8-88524-656-9 (paperback)
ISBN: 979-8-88524-657-6 (ebook)

Photo Credits
Images are courtesy of Shutterstock.com. With thanks to Getty Images, Thinkstock Photo and iStockphoto. Cover – StockImageFactory.com, bestv, nevodka, p4–5 –Happy Stock Photo, LightField Studios, p6–7 – Aina Cas, NagornyiSergiy, p8–9 – niderlander, Olga Klochanko, p10–11 –344512847, siamionau pavel. P12 - NagornyiSergiy, Lightfield Studios, Olga Klochanko, Aina Cas.

About Reading

When we read
a book, we go
from left to
right, like this:

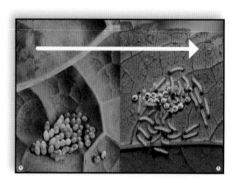

Some books
just have
pictures,
like this:

Some books
have words
and pictures,
like this:

Which of these steps comes last?

Close the book and flip it over to read Chinese New Year!